Fight the Good Fight

How to Get Back Up
When Life Knocks You Down

Tony Tucker

&

JoAnne E. Gillespie

Fight the Good Fight

Copyright © 2015 by Tony Tucker & JoAnne E. Gillespie

All rights reserved. In accordance with the U.S. Copyright Act of 1976, the scanning, uploading, and electronic sharing of any part of this book without the permission of the publisher is unlawful piracy and theft of the author's intellectual property. If you would like to use material from this book (other than for review purposes) prior written permission must be obtained by contacting the publisher. Thank you for your support of the author's rights.

Published by:
Gillespie Digital Media Group
241 S. 78th Street
Tampa, FL 33619
www.gillespiedigitalmediagroup.com
The publisher is not responsible for websites (or their content) that are not owned by the publisher.

ISBN-13: 978-0692495452

Formatted by: Wild Seas Formatting

For Worldwide Distribution
Printed in the United States of America

First Edition 2015

DEDICATION

I would like to dedicate my first book to my mom, Mattie Tucker. My mother has been a solid influence in my life for as long as I can remember. She has been there for me when no one else was there for me. My mom raised her three children alone after my dad left the home and we never went without anything we needed as children. There are no words to explain a mother's love. I am her first born and there is a bond that cannot be explained with mere words.

My mom has been a bedrock of strength for me. It was a huge disappointment to my mother to see me in the depths of despair and given over to the throngs of addiction. But my mother loved and took care of me through all of the ups and downs in my life. In her eyes I am still her baby son and she loves me unconditionally. I am the man that I am today because of my mother's love, encouragement, and strength. My mother, Mattie Tucker, introduced me to the Lord and gave me a solid foundation to build upon. I did not always implement the things that she taught me but in my darkest hours the foundation that my mother put in my life came to the forefront and enabled me to get back up when life knocked me down.

ACKNOWLEDGEMENTS

Every accomplishment in life is the result of the contribution of many individuals who both directly and indirectly share their gifts, their talents, and their wisdom with us all. This project and my life are no exception. My life story would have never been on the pages of any book had it not been for the tireless commitment and efforts of JoAnne Gillespie who spent countless hours writing this book and assuring its publication. There have also been a number of people on my journey who contributed to my well being in one way or another and I want to take this opportunity to give a special thanks to Pastor Robert Johnson, Carlo Colucci, Gary Gittleson and my friend Shelly Finkel. I would never have entered into a professional boxing career had in not been for the training I received from my father, Robert Tucker, so I want to thank him for his many years of dedication and service. Likewise, I am grateful and appreciative to Antoine Jackson and Andrea LaToya Williams for taking time to edit this project. Most of all I am ever so grateful to the Lord for preserving my life and giving me the strength to get back up when life knocked me down and for the opportunity to share my journey with you.

FOREWORD

Over the course of my career I have had the privilege of managing a number of professional boxers. One of those boxers is former World Heavyweight Boxing Champion, **Tony "TNT" Tucker**. I saw great potential in Tony as a boxer and admired his integrity as a man. However, there were many elements that came into play that I knew could potentially derail his boxing career. As his manager, I went to great lengths to try to assist Tony when he was faced with battles outside of the ring as I knew that he had the potential to be a great champion.

I was in his life before he got into those struggles and I had the opportunity to come back into his life during the time he was battling with addiction. Boxing in and of itself is brutal and coupled together with substance abuse was a two-edged sword that would cut very deep. It was my intent, as his manger and friend, to get him into rehab and to get his career back on track. Addiction is brutal and it turned out to be unrelenting.

Tony "TNT" Tucker was a great boxer who has overcome many adversities. He has faced many obstacles in his career as well as his personal life. Oftentimes, the greatest roadblocks were from those closest to him.
I am proud and honored that **Tony "TNT" Tucker** is sharing his story with the world. It is compelling and forthright. It is very rare that anyone shares this much intimate detail about

their life and is as honest about their addiction.

Tony "TNT" Tucker has proved that he is indeed a champion in more ways than one in and out of the boxing ring. I watched him through the years and always hoped he would make something of himself. Needless to say, in the manner of a true champion, **Tony "TNT" Tucker** got back up when life knocked him down and is reaching out to others to show them the way, instill hope, and impart strength.

The mark of a true champion.

Shelly Finkel
Chairman of Strategy and Development of SFX

ENDORSEMENTS

Tony Tucker and I go way back. My father took me to Detroit in the early part of my career to spar with Tony. We were two young, up and coming fighters---driven by a dream. As fate would have it, we ended up fighting years later for the IBF Title. Tony proved to be a better fighter that night, defeated me, and his dream came true. Still driven by the dream, I came back and won three years later. From our early sparring days in Detroit, to him defeating me for the title, those experiences made me a better fighter and helped me become the Heavyweight Champion of the world. We fulfilled our dreams and our father's visions.
James "Buster" Douglas
Former World Heavyweight Boxing Champion

Mr. Tony "TNT" Tucker is a former heavyweight champion of the world. A man that I have looked up to over the years. A man that knew how to use his size and reach to his advantage and a man that displayed great character in and out of the ring. Mr. Tucker I thank you for being one of the pioneers that paved the road for me in this long abusive sport we call boxing. From one champ to another, may you fulfill all your goals and dreams.
Michael Moorer
Former World Heavyweight & World Light-Heavyweight Boxing Champion

What I want you to know about Tony "TNT" Tucker is that Tony was a great fighter who became a Heavyweight Champion of the World. But even better than that, Tony is a champion on how he treats people! Tony is one of the most soft-spoken and genuine people I know and I am glad and privileged to call him a friend.
Winky Wright
Undisputed Junior Middleweight Champion

TABLE OF CONTENTS

Preface x
Prelude xi
Introduction xiii
Chapter 1- Beginnings 1
Chapter 2- Bullies: Entering the Ring of Life 3
Chapter 3- Family Challenges 6
Chapter 4- First Time in the Ring 7
Chapter 5- Boxing as a Career 8
Chapter 6- Rolling with the Punches 10
Chapter 7- Working on the Railroad 12
Chapter 8- Focused 14
Chapter 9- Return Home with Fame 16
Chapter 10- Globetrotter 18
Chapter 11- Entering the Professional Ring 21
Chapter 12- Becoming Famous 23
Chapter 13- Poor Management 25
Chapter 14 On the Road to the Championship 27
Chapter 15- Preparing for Mike Tyson 31
Chapter 16- The Tyson Fight 34
Chapter 17- The Pretty White Devil 38
Chapter 18- Downward Descent 41
Chapter 19- Functioning Addict 43
Chapter 20- You Quit a Thousand Times 45
Chapter 21: The First Payment 47
Chapter 22- Boxing During my Dark Days 51
Chapter 23- Lennox Lewis Handicap Match 56
Chapter 24- The Fallout 59

Chapter 25- Still Taking its Toll 61
Chapter 26- Counting the Costs 64
Chapter 27- The End of It All 67
Chapter 28- Exit Orders 70
Chapter 29- A Light in the Darkness 72
Chapter 30- Back at it Again....................................... 73
Chapter 31- I Looked Up and Got Up......................... 75
Chapter 32- How to Get Back Up When Life
       Knocks You Down 78
Contact Information 81

PREFACE

I was a World Heavyweight Boxing Champion and a gold medalist, not once but twice. I have been in the ring and went toe to toe with the best of the best. Contrary to ignorant stereotypes and quiet as it is kept, drugs do not discriminate. *Tony "TNT" Tucker* is an elite member of World Heavyweight Boxing Champions, yet here I was reduced to the lowest of the low. Here I was in a place that some of you will only identify with from the movies or something you saw scripted on television. But then there are those who will read the pages of this book and identify wholeheartedly with the pain of addiction on a more personal level, either as one who is in the throngs of addiction right now or as one who has gone through it and was able to walk away. There will also be those who will read the pages of this book who have family members deeply entrenched in the depths of drug addiction for whom you pray and weep constantly. It appears that they are helpless and hopeless. To this group, I want to be the one to encourage you to never give up on your loved ones, friends, or family. Allow me to be the one to instill a sense of hope in you as you stand in the gap for your loved one.
Tony "TNT" Tucker

Life rarely goes along as most of us would like for it to in our vivid imaginations. The perfect script would not include any ups and downs, pain, anguish, losses or disappointments. However, it is the combination of these things and much more that mold us into the unique individuals that we are in this life. It has been my greatest joy to convey what was in the heart *of Tony "TNT" Tucker* in sharing his life story with you. It is very up close, intimate, and personal. It is the story of victory and defeat. It is the story of ups and downs. Ins and outs. Gains and losses. It is the story of a man who reached the heights of victory and experienced the depths of despair. It is the story of a man who one day looked up and then got up. Ultimately, our desire is that Tony's story will encourage you to **Fight the Good Fight** and show you **How to Get Back Up When Life Knocks You Down**.
JoAnne E. Gillespie

Prelude

"Dammit, what is all of that noise!?" The sounds of sirens were blaring from the street below as helicopters whipped the air while hovering over the hotel. "Ah, shit!" I thought to myself, "I'm busted... Let me lie here for a few minutes and see if they go away. Hell... No, they are coming to get *me*!" I fumbled my way to the bathroom and flushed all of my dope down the toilet. Therefore, when they burst in the room to get me, there will be nothing incriminating there, no evidence of drugs or anything. Everything— all of my drugs that I had bought for my private binge while holed up in the hotel on Crenshaw Boulevard in Los Angeles— went down the toilet.

I jumped in the bed, threw the covers on me, and waited anxiously, pretending to be an unassuming statue. "If they found me, maybe they'll be sympathetic, seeing me in such a peaceful and vulnerable position," I thought. I stayed perfectly in place for a few more terrifying minutes that seemed like hours, and then decided I would make my way outside. Yet nothing happened. No one kicked in the door to my hotel room, no guns were pointed at me, and no one manhandled me to the floor.

When I finally did get outside I was greeted by pandemonium. People were *everywhere* in the streets! Looters were running with carts full from ransacked stores. A known homeless man also partook in the chaos and asked me if I wanted to buy some tampons! Nothing, not even the most mundane, was spared. What the hell was going on in the streets of Los Angeles? What was happening right in front of my eyes? Little did I know, it was the beginning of the Rodney King Riots. It had nothing to do with *me*, as the binge had made me believe.

Still in a stupor, my phone rang. It was my wife, Kim, calling to tell me that we needed to get out of Los Angeles and head back to Las Vegas. However, the only things that were on my mind were the fact that I had just flushed ALL of my dope down the toilet for nothing, and where I could I get some more, and when.

The use of crack cocaine made me paranoid ALL of the time. *What kind of sense would it make for helicopters and all of those police to be looking for me?* I was not a big-time drug dealer; I wasn't even that championship boxer anymore. I had been reduced to a "crackhead," a "rockhead," a "baser." In other words, I was reduced to a common crack addict.

Introduction

My name is *Tony "TNT" Tucker*. I was a National AAU Light Heavyweight Champion. I held the USBA Heavyweight title. I was a two-time NABF Heavyweight Champion. I held the California State Heavyweight Title. I was a gold medalist at the Pan-American Games and a gold medalist in the World Cup at Light Heavyweight. Probably most notably, I am a former IBF Heavyweight World Champion.

I was ducked by boxing greats Michael Spinks and George Foreman. I went toe-to-toe with great boxers such as Mike Tyson and Lennox Lewis to a standstill. Through two decades, I held a 58-7 record against top-notch competition, including: Jimmy Young, Buster Douglas, Mike Tyson, Orlin Norris (twice), Oliver McCall, Lennox Lewis, Henry Akinwande, Herbie Hide, Bruce Seldon, and John Ruiz.

I am also a champion against crack cocaine addiction…

You hear about stories of romanticized success all the time on the news and social media. What about my latest victory? It is the story that no one wants to tell: the story of drugs and addiction, the dark side of fame and fortune. It is the story that takes great athletes from the height of victory and plunges them into the depths of despair. It is the story that leads a man to find himself in drug holes and seedy hotels plagued by paranoia. It is the story that started off with one hit of a pipe in the glitz of Beverly Hills and ended with squalor in a scorched apartment.

This is a story of untold anguish, inner turmoil and indescribable pain. This *was* my story, but one day I looked up, held the hand of God, and got up. I am Tony "TNT" Tucker, and I am sharing my story with you: up-close, intimate, detailed, painful and very personal.

Chapter 1- Beginnings

It was a cold and blistery day in Grand Rapids, Michigan on December 27th, 1958. That day, I, Anthony Craig Tucker, made my entrance into the world. Not long after bringing me home from the hospital, my dad threw me on the bed and said, "He is going to be my champion." My mother said that she just freaked out, because I was only a newborn baby and my father was handling me a bit rough.

My dad, Robert Tucker, was a fighter. I remember vividly the first time I saw him in the ring when I was about five years old. My dad had a lot of friends who would come and hang out around our house all the time and encourage him. He was "the man." During those times, I would observe those guys supporting my dad and giving him so many accolades. The attention given to my dad made me proud that Robert Tucker was my father. I was excited just by watching their interaction with him. My father seemed to be pretty famous around Grand Rapids, and I was ultimately proud to be his son.

Robert Tucker said that he always wanted to be a heavyweight boxing champion. There was a time when I was a little boy that I remember sitting with my grandfather at a venue where my dad was boxing. My dad got knocked down by his opponent. My grandfather leaned over to me and told me, "Go tell your daddy to get up." Without question, I headed over to the ring where my dad was boxing and started screaming at the top of my lungs, "Get up, Daddy, get up, Daddy, get up, Daddy!!" Like the true fighter that Robert Tucker was, he responded to my screams and got up and proceeded to defeat his opponent. Robert Tucker had a reputation in Grand Rapids of being a tough guy and a great boxer; he didn't disappoint.

You see growing up, I watched all of the superheroes on television and was always fascinated by the characters in the cartoons. In the same light, I was always so proud of my dad, because everybody knew who "Tucker" was in the community, and I wanted to be just like him. I looked up to him. He was the person I wanted to emulate. He was the person that I wanted to be like when I grew up. My dad *was* my superhero.

Chapter 2- Bullies: Entering the Ring of Life

It's no surprise that I was introduced to boxing at a very young age. I must have been about 3 or 4 years old. It began with my dad showing me boxing moves such as how to jab, left hooks and different combinations. At times when a lot of my dad's friends would hang at our house, he would have me come down to the living room and tell me to start throwing all sorts of combinations (boxing sequences). I took note of all of the applause and attention that my dad received when I showcased the boxing moves that he taught me. I also noticed the joy and excitement in his eyes. This made me happy, too. Those in-home exhibitions were my first introduction to boxing.

I remember as a little kid in grade school that there was a Hispanic kid named George who used to chase me home every single day after school. I don't know why I was so terrified of this kid, but I just know that he would bully me and chase me home every single day. One day, my dad saw him chasing me and told me if he ever saw me running away again from that kid that he would whoop my behind! However, that threat from my father did little at all to stop me from running home after school. I was completely terrified of this kid. I was so terrified of this bully that I would rather face my dad and the extension cord rather than face George. Like clockwork, this kid would wait for me to get out of school every day so he could taunt me and chase me home.

But I recall on this one particular day, my little brother, Donnie, and I were together and the bully chased us both. It so happened that he caught my brother as I continued to run around the corner of the block on the way home, seeking safety. I contemplated as I was running towards home whether I should keep running or go help my brother. Suddenly, I paused. My decision was made clear when I heard the bully's fists hitting Donnie's flesh. Instantly, the love for my brother caused me to overcome my fear of George. I turned around and ran back to where he was attacking Donnie, and I pushed George to the ground and he fell backwards. All of a sudden the bully I feared for so long jumped up and started running away. The tables had turned, and I started chasing him home after that, and when I would catch him, I would beat his ass, gaining retribution for what seemed like years of torment. This is when I found out that some of the boxing skills that my father taught me really worked.

During my grade school years, we went to a lot of different schools, and I would always spot the bullies. I knew that at some point, some or all of them would come after me. Well into my adolescent years, I was quiet and shy and did not mess with anyone, yet the bullies always spotted me for some reason. They would come after me faithfully, and when they did, I would use the techniques that my father taught me about boxing, the same ones I used on George, and beat their ass, too. I was not a bully and did not pick on anyone, but if they picked on me I would go to work on them. I can remember knocking a kid's tooth out that bullied me using the techniques I learned at home.

Through the years I built up a reputation. Everywhere we went, everyone would say that Tony Tucker could *fight*. Some of my best matches and training were gained through experience, growing up fighting people in school and in the streets. In fact, most of my matches, before I really got into the boxing ring, were on the playground or after school. These were my training grounds.

A lot of the fights I got into in those days were to protect Donnie. For one thing, my brother would instigate fights by telling whoever was picking on him, "I bet you can't beat my brother!" Needless to say, I had to defend my honor and my brother.

For a while, groups of guys would try to jump on me

after school. Since they could not take me on one at a time, the bullies eventually resorted to ganging up on me. One time in particular, Donnie spotted a group that was waiting for me as the final bell rang. I told him to hurry home and tell Mom about this group of guys that were coming after me. Donnie was headed home and my mom saw him coming down the street, kicking a can with no sense of urgency. So much for rushing! When he finally arrived home, he told my mother about the boys and their plan to jump me after school. Needless to say, she made her way to the school in the nick of time, and all issues were resolved nonviolently on this occasion.

Another time, my good friends Mike Lagrone, Jerome, Jerome's sister, Velma, and I were at Jefferson School. All of the "tough guys" at the school wanted to jump me. So Mike, Jerome, Velma, and I went back-to-back fighting these guys off. Mike, Jerome and Velma were my "road dogs," best friends. At one time I even had a serious crush on Velma, but it did not work out. We tried to date, but I was too much like a brother to her. Those were the days… We stuck together, and some of my fondest memories of those years were made spending time with my good friends and road dogs.

Chapter 3- Family Challenges

I was young when my parents separated. The separation of my mother and father had a major effect on me, because I wanted my family to stay intact. I was a kid that refused to be denied, and as long as my dad was in Grand Rapids, I was determined to see him.

I never saw any violence in our home, but I could hear my parents arguing, and I did not want my dad to hurt my mom. It was a great concern to me, because I knew that he could, being a trained fighter. When my parents finally went their separate ways, my dad told me one day that he may have to go to jail because of failure to pay child support. I went home and begged my mother not to put my dad in jail. Of course, at that time, I did not understand all the ramifications of child support or the implications as it related to my mom receiving money for our care. I just knew that I did not want my dad to go to jail. My mother never pursued child support and managed to take care of three children on her own without us ever lacking anything in terms of food, clothes, or shelter. My mother was and still remains a very strong black woman of whom I am very proud.

I have five siblings. From my dad and mom, Mattie Tucker, I have one brother, Donnie, and one sister, Mitzi. I also have another brother, Staci, and another sister, Tonya, who my dad fathered with Dorothy Mayweather, Floyd Mayweather, Sr.'s sister. Additionally, I have another brother, Josh, who my dad fathered with a woman he was seeing in Detroit. In essence, *my poppa was a rolling stone, and truly wherever he laid his hat was his home.*

Chapter 4- First Time in the Ring

The first time that I was in the ring was with Fred Leonard at an exhibition. I threw one of the punching combinations that my dad had taught me as a young boy. That particular combination worked, and the crowd started roaring. I instantly became addicted to it, because all of these people were cheering for *me*, Tony Tucker. From that point on, I started building a reputation and suddenly became engulfed into this secret boxing world. It was my world. In this world, I felt an unexplainable high that made me feel special when I was fighting in front of a crowd of people, and I loved it.

After that first exhibition, my dad accepted an opportunity to run a boxing gym in Grand Rapids. This gym is where Floyd Mayweather, Sr.— who was about 15 or 16 years old at that time— and all of the "tough guys" who were on the street, would come to box. "Tucker" had to get them in shape, because if they were fighting the white guys, they were going to have to be in good shape, because all of the white boxers were in very good shape. Floyd, Sr. was a big Muhammad Ali fan and could do all of the shuffles and different moves when we were coming up. I was at the gym training with all of these guys, and they saw me doing the moves that my dad taught me, and they knew I could do the job in the ring. (Floyd, Sr., of course, would go on to father Floyd Mayweather, Jr., a boxing superstar and champion.)

During the time when I was in the gym working like the older guys, I would fight in different exhibitions. I also was privileged to fight in the Junior Olympics when I was 14 or 15 years old, and I won some of the fights. At 16, I fought in the Golden Gloves series and became the State Champion.

Chapter 5- Boxing as a Career

I never really gave thought to boxing long term. As a matter of fact, boxing would not have been my first choice *as a sport*, let alone a career. I really liked football, basketball, and baseball. I could hit a baseball out of the ball park. However, my father introduced me to boxing, and it was a way for me to have a relationship and spend quality time with him. After all, my father was my superhero and my trainer, so naturally, I pursued boxing.

The Golden Gloves National Tournament was the first national boxing competition that I ever attended. That particular year, the competition was held in Honolulu, Hawaii. Attending the national competition was one thing, but this would be my very first time boarding an aircraft. The first thing I wanted to get done before boarding the plane was be baptized.

I have always had a knowledge and a certain respect for God. Well, I knew I didn't want to go to hell. As selfish as it was, I was concerned about my own soul at this point, so I needed to get baptized. In order to fulfil this mission, I attended a Pentecostal Church in Grand Rapids, Michigan where I was able to be baptized. Once I had been baptized, I felt safe about boarding the plane to head to Hawaii. The flight from Grand Rapids, Michigan to Honolulu, Hawaii was the start of a journey that I could have never imagined.

The Golden Glove National Tournament, having been my first tournament at a national level, had me extremely nervous. I was lucky enough to have won my first fight at the tournament, but my second fight was not as favorable. During the second fight, I did not give my all, and ultimately my opponent defeated me in the ring. This loss wasn't devastating and did not cause me to feel sorry for myself, because I looked at my 17-year-old self and saw that I had competed in a *nation-wide* competition and had successfully traveled from Grand Rapids to Honolulu, attempting to take a chance on my boxing career. The remainder of my time in Hawaii was spent enjoying the sights and scenery of such a beautiful state while looking at all the pretty girls. I really enjoyed the rest of that trip and had not realized how beautiful the world really was. Up until that point I had a very limited worldview.

The year after the trip to Honolulu, I won so many titles around Grand Rapids in my weight class as a "light heavyweight," which has a 178-pound limitation. As I began to reach 179 and 180 pounds, I had to move to the regular heavyweight boxing category, which was a Grand Rapids boxing stipulation. In boxing you must move up or down. Since I could not move down in weight class, I had no choice but to move to the heavyweight boxing category. I did not understand all of the complications of the boxing weight classes, but it was something I had to adhere to in order to participate in boxing.

There was a mandated weight class change forced on me by the City of Grand Rapids, I was neither physically or mentally ready to fight heavyweight. I was a "light" 180 pounds facing opponents well over 220 pounds. Additionally, it did not help that I was a little shy. My confidence level was not there, I did not feel like I was big enough, and I was still a little timid. Even so, I was still motivated. When I lost at the nationals, I told my father, *"Daddy, I am going to do whatever you want me to do, because I really want this."* I decided that I really wanted to fight to win.

Chapter 6- Rolling with the Punches

It was one guy that my father took me to see in the Nationals before I ever fought in a national tournament. When we arrived at the venue, there was this *huge* guy there who had muscles *everywhere*, a real body-builder type. My father said to me, "I am going to show you something." My dad went to the big muscle-bound guy and said to him, "You are a big guy, and I bet you knock people out easily." Of course, the big guy agreed. My dad had brought along some balloons with him to this fight to teach me a boxing lesson. "Tucker" asked muscle man if he could burst a balloon by hitting it. So the big guy, confident as he was with arms like a statue, swung on the balloon as hard as he could with blows that could have easily destroyed any man. And yet... he could not burst the balloon.

My dad told me to pay close attention. The lesson "Tucker" taught me was never to take the full effect of a punch. He taught me how to *roll* with the punch like a balloon, rather than taking the punch's full force. The balloon was not stationary when hit; it moved (rolled) with the flow of force from the punch, deflecting some force and absorbing the rest. If it was stationary and rigid and tried to *resist* the punch, it would have popped just like if you hold a balloon in place on the ground and stomp on it. Of course, there is an art to learning how to roll with the punch and not get a neck injury. So, as big as he was and as hard as he could hit, he could not burst those balloons, because the balloons could roll with the punches. That was a very valuable lesson that my dad taught me.

Additionally, I learned that you have to be able to roll with the punches in life just like you have to learn how to roll with the punches in the ring. Although, I did not learn the lesson of rolling with the punches in life until much later on...

Also, you cannot get in the ring and be scared of getting hit, because *you are going to get hit.* It is all about how you take the punch. Boxing is the "hurt business." If you are scared of getting hit, you are going to get hit more. As far as taking the *hardest* of hits, I really was not the fighter who got hit a lot, but if I did, it would put me in defense mode. One of my father's defense strategies was to not get hit! It was always, "*Hit and not get hit!*" He drilled that into me over and over. All of these lessons took me a very long way.

Chapter 7- Working on the Railroad

At one time, I worked at the railroad. Like the tale of John Henry, I had a sledgehammer driving spikes into the wooden railroad ties, connecting the rails to the wood. At that time, the only boxing training I could get was geared toward the USA Boxing Team. Even though this was the only job available while I was preparing to box, the physical activity built much needed muscles. My training and work prepared me for the opportunity to fight on the U.S. Boxing Team against Poland.

Here I was, a kid from Grand Rapids scared to fly to another state, now on an international flight to another country. Not only had my confidence for flying improved, but my skills in the ring improved as well. I seemed to have come a long way since my loss in Honolulu. I won the match in Poland, a world away, so successfully that it seemed uneventful. I knocked the kid out!

Pat Nappi, an Olympic head coach, told me, "When you get to this level, you are going to love it!" He was referring to the U.S.A. boxing team. I made up my mind right then and there that I wanted this more than anything, and I told my dad again that I would do any type of training so I could be at that level. Pat Nappi was the one who made me want to soar and reach my full potential.

After the match in Poland, I quit the railroad and started training for fights full time. I prepared for the Amateur Athletic Union (AAU) and made the decision that I wanted to keep winning. Rick Jester, a national winner, was my next opponent. He was from the Kronk Boxing team, and we were fighting for the Michigan State Boxing Title. I boxed the shit out of him and won that fight. This particular win took my confidence level to another level. When I beat Rick Jester, I knew I was ready. I was the state AAU champion and was poised to be a national champion.

The Nationals were in Louisiana, and I was in very good a shape. I ran 5 to 7 miles every day to make the light heavyweight category. Even though I won the National AAU Light Heavyweight Championship, the Pan-American Games were also that year. Before I could fight in the Pan-American Games, I had to go the Olympic training camp and participate in the box offs. After that was the Pan-American trials, of which I had to win in order to be apart the Pan-American Olympic team. I won the trials and was officially on the team. Only the best of the best went to the Pan-American Games.

Chapter 8- Focused

During the time of the Pan-American Games, I was so focused. I refused not to leave without the gold medal. *I refused to lose!* At the Pan-American Games, I was chosen to fight a guy from Cuba named Sixto Soria. Soria fought Leon Spinks in the 1976 Summer Olympics in Montreal, Canada for the gold medal. Sixto Soria lost to Leon Spinks in that match. Regardless, these guys were pros fighting us amateurs.

During the first two rounds of the fight, I kept dodging the right and hitting him with my left hook. Then, in the 3rd round when I slipped his right, he elbowed me out of frustration, because he could not hit me. This was a slick, old pro move. He cut me over the eye, but I pleaded with doctors to not stop the fight, since it was the last round. They allowed me continue the fight, and I went on to win by decision. I got my eye stitched up, and I had four more matches to endure with a cut eye. Of course, this meant that I was in danger of getting hit and re-opening the wound.

All the moves and techniques that my dad taught me went into full effect: hit and not get hit, roll with the punches, and ducking and dodging. Now, I was knocking everybody out and looking for punches that would land. The last guy who I boxed in the Games was from Puerto Rico, and I needed to defeat him for the gold medal at the 1979 Pan-American Games. I knew going in that I had to win it all. I was determined to win it all. I had to stay focused, and I refused to lose. In the end, I walked away with the gold medal.

My scale of resolve stemmed from Pat Nappi's words of inspiration: I DID love it at this level of competition! When I won the gold medal, not only did I become the best boxer in the nation for my weight class, *I was the best in the world.*

After I won the Pan-American Games and was declared the gold medalist, my next happiest moment was when I stepped onto the winner platform, and they played the National Anthem. I had such a sense of pride as an American. I was not just an African American boxer from Grand Rapids, Michigan but also a very proud member of the United States Olympic Boxing Team. This was one of the happiest moments in my life.

Chapter 9- Return Home with Fame

When I arrived back in Grand Rapids, I was like an overnight superstar! The newspaper and the television people flocked to my house for interviews. My mother brought me a brand new van with letters "TNT" on the back wheel cover. Do those of you old enough remember the vans with the swivel seats and shag carpet? This was one of them! Everybody knew who I was in Grand Rapids, Michigan. Now, Tony "*TNT*" Tucker was born and became a true local celebrity.

My fame did not evade my personal life at this point. Returning from the Pan-American Games, there was another woman besides my mom who I had to come back home to in Grand Rapids. She was 24 years old and the mother of five children. I had moved in with her prior to traveling. At that time, I was every bit her man at 17 years old, and those children were every bit my children; no one could have told me anything different. I was "the man," or at least I thought so at the time. My newfound fame and notoriety did not go over too well with my woman. For some odd reason, every time that I would go to the house, there seemed to be another man leaving through the back door while I was entering the front door. Eventually, it became clear and I was replaced by someone else. This event was like a jab to the gut, crushing my tender, naïve heart. Nevertheless, it also freed me to venture out and enjoy my newfound fame while experimenting with girls closer to my age.

During the next few years, I spent a lot of time hanging out with Roger Mayweather and discovered how famous I really was. When we would go into a place Roger told me to tell them who I was, and I would introduce myself as "*Tony 'TNT' Tucker*". This was my first real exposure to fame and recognition. This initial shot of fame was intoxicating. When people realized who I was, a famous boxer, I received many a-welcoming responses and all of the perks. Of course, being a young man, this was all foreign to me, but nonetheless enjoyable. Especially the *perks!*

Chapter 10- Globetrotter

The Boxing World Cup came up four to five months after the Pan-American Games. Needless to say, I was in the gym training diligently. At that time, a young Floyd Mayweather, Jr., was present while his dad and I were training. I remember him trying to do the jump rope like his dad. We had some great times at that gym; it holds a special place in my mind. Some of my fondest memories were of me hanging out with my dad and some really great guys including Floyd Mayweather, Sr. and Roger Mayweather. This was the gym where I trained to prepare for my newly decided career in boxing. It was a very humble beginning.

I went on to win the gold medal at the Boxing World Cup. Amazingly, I was the Pan-American Gold Medalist *and* the Boxing World Cup Gold Medalist. These two victories positioned me to be a celebrity all over the world.

After the World Cup, my dad and I made a trip to California, because my dad wanted to check out Harold Smith who ran the Muhammad Ali Amateur Boxing Team in California. My dad and I went on a three-day road trip from Grand Rapids, Michigan to Los Angeles, California in the van that my mom had bought for me. Tony "TNT" Tucker and Robert Tucker were on the move across the country.

When we finally arrived in Los Angeles, we stopped at the gym and met Harold Smith, President of the Muhammad Ali Amateur Boxing team. Harold Smith took us to Muhammad Ali's house, and Mr. Ali himself informed us that he wanted me to be on his boxing team. My only apprehension was that amateur fighters did not get paid. My dad and I were told that if I moved to Los Angeles, I would get housing, a car and $1,000-a-month allowance. So my dad took the offer and we moved to California. Ultimately, it turned out to be a bad move, because I was not fighting as much as I did in Michigan.

Later, after moving to California, I received an offer to fight on the U.S. Olympic Boxing team in Germany. My dad and I accepted that offer. The U.S. Olympic Boxing team went to Germany, and I had to fight as a heavyweight. Unfortunately, I did not do a very good job. I lost by decision. From there, the U.S. Olympic Boxing team traveled to Poland. Like in Germany, I lost to what seemed like the Polish home field advantage.

Our U.S. Olympic Boxing team flew back to the United States and landed in New York. When we arrived home, there was another U.S. boxing team preparing to head overseas. I contemplated whether I should go back overseas to redeem myself by defeating the European guys that I lost to previously. Ultimately, something told me not to go back. Instead, I went to California, got a few things from my place, and headed back to Michigan. I was homesick and wanted to see my mom.

When I finally arrived at my mother's home, she raced to greet me at the door. She kept kissing and hugging me and thanking the Lord that I was alive. I was confused; I could not figure out why my mom was kissing me so much. After all of the warm embraces, she told she thought that I was on the plane that crashed. *"What plane?!"* I thought. She explained that it was that Polish Airlines flight, the very same one that I contemplated boarding just hours before. The plane crashed while attempting to land in Warsaw, killing all 87 people on board including 22 members of the United States Boxing team. In fact, it was the *very same jet* that had brought me and the other members of the first team back to the United States! All the other members that had tried to return to Poland were now *dead*. A lot of those guys were my close friends. Coach Tom "Sarge" Johnson, whom I loved dearly, was on that plane. I was in disbelief and crushed to hear that news. Again, I was struck by an unsuspecting sharp blow to the gut. It was truly a very sad day for me personally and in boxing history.

Moments after hearing the tragic news from my mother,

newspaper and television reporters started showing up to her front door. They descended on her house like vultures, because they believed I was on that plane that killed members of the team. Grateful that my life was spared, my heart still ached for my fellow boxers and team members.

Chapter 11- Entering the Professional Ring

After all of the issues relating to the plane crash settled down, a lot of boxers were discouraged, because the 1980 Summer Olympics hosted in Moscow had been boycotted. Politics and sports intersected due to the 1979 Soviet invasion of Afghanistan and the Soviets' refusal to withdraw from Afghanistan. My long-awaited Olympic dreams were shattered as was my chance to win a gold medal in the 1980 Summer Olympics. It was, to say the least, one of the greatest disappointments in my career.

Shortly after the 1980 Summer Olympic boycott, I started my professional boxing career after compiling an amateur record of 115 wins to 6 losses. When I turned pro, I received a handsome signing bonus. The signing bonus was more than I had ever had in cash in my young life. My first purchase was a Lincoln Continental. I was about 21 years old and seemed to be rolling in dough. I strutted into the car dealership and signed over my whole check to the dealer and left instructions to hold it until I came back. I was young and very naïve. My accountant straightened everything out, because he knew that the dealer had taken full advantage of me. The only reason I purchased the car was to attend a big event in town later that night. I wanted to roll up in my brand new Lincoln Continental and impress the onlookers. Once again, I was "the man," feeling on top, or at least I thought so in my own mind.

My first professional fight was televised on national TV via NBC. Several of the other fighters that were on the Olympic team were also contracted to the same promoters and managers that I had and were shown on TV as well.

These bouts were part of a television program known as "Tomorrow's Champions." My first professional fight was held on November 1, 1980 at the Caesars Tahoe in Nevada. I fought against Chuck Gardner, and I won by a knockout. I was well on my way as a professional boxer. After my first professional fight, I moved forward with a long undefeated stretch.

As a professional boxer, I signed up with the famed Kronk Gym out of Detroit, Michigan where I trained with the legendary Emanuel Steward. Famed boxer Thomas "The Hit Man" Hearns fought for Kronk Gym and put it on the map. Being associated with Kronk Gym was good for me, for it provided me with an opportunity to receive coaching from well-known boxing trainers in the world of boxing.

Chapter 12- Becoming Famous

Winning my first televised fight on NBC amplified my former gold-medal notoriety and fame which spring boarded me into the Professional Boxing Arena. As a pro boxer in Detroit, Michigan, I reconnected with my first cousin, Donald Herron, my best friend and road dog for many years. Donald challenged my training regimen to the point where I could do 1000 push-ups per day. These workouts increased my punching power and made me stronger as a heavyweight. Donald was a very important part of my life and an integral part of advancing my boxing career.

After my initial professional fight, I was signed with Bob Arum who became my promoter. Shelly Finkel and Lou Duva were my managers. I started boxing regularly. Sometimes, I would fight under the Bob Arum umbrella and other times under Kronk Gym. However, eventually, the trio broke up. The split occurred after Finkel had a supposed fall-out with Arum. I was not privileged to the details, but I got hit with a hard blow from the marketing standpoint, because that break-up affected my fights being televised.

My dad, who guided everything about my boxing career, decided to leave both Finkel and Arum and go with Cedric Kushner who traditionally promoted rock musicians. My dad thought that he could negotiate with this promoter better, because Kushner did not know much about boxing which would allow my dad to maintain control. Ultimately, my dad re-positioned himself as my manager.

Having my dad function as my manager was a fatal mistake. Eventually, he would micromanage my boxing career. For instance, I was a well-known and undefeated heavyweight and had the opportunity to fight Larry Holmes in the place of Michael Spinks. But because my dad was my manager, I could not capitalize on that chance, so that fight never came to fruition. In the meantime, there were a long string of victories for me in the ring. I was winning one fight after another, and my professional boxing career was well underway. But you can't avoid being hit forever. This came in the form of the fight against Danny Sutton. The match was held at the Hyatt Regency Hotel in Atlantic City, New Jersey, and the bout was declared "no contest." In that fight, I sustained a knee injury that derailed me and kept me out of the ring for well over a year.

During this time in my life, I was in love with a girl from New York, Channel Florio. She is the mother of my oldest daughter, Francesca Florio. I travelled back and forth from Detroit to New York and lived in New York for a while where I was receiving therapy for my injured knee.

For a while, I was exercising my knee regularly and then returned to training; however, my knee kept giving out on me due to torn tendons and ligaments. Eventually, I was forced to go to California to receive surgery on my knee which put me out of the boxing ring for a while longer.

Chapter 13- Poor Management

After I fully recuperated from my knee injury, I went back into training mode in Detroit, Michigan. When I got back in the ring, I was raring to go. Unfortunately, my manager, *my dad*, did not advocate for the big-name fights for me. Because of my strong loyalty to my dad, I allowed him to manage everything about my boxing career even though I was beginning to recognize that he was becoming a detriment to me personally and professionally. But at that time, I did not know anything else; all I knew was how to box and to trust those closest to me with every other aspect of my career. Of course, my dad knew everything about training and the *art* of boxing, but regrettably, he knew nothing about the *business* of boxing, a fact that would prove to be a serious liability much later on in my career.

After my knee healed up, I had a few more fights scheduled. Luckily, I found some business favor with these fights. Some of these fights were on the undercard of mainstream boxers and matches like Thomas Hearns and Sugar Ray Leonard. This was a step in the right direction. Later, I would fight on the same card as Roberto Duran and Marvin Hagler. These were all step-up fights, matches that would both get me more exposure as well as test my abilities against stronger opponents.

For instance, my bout with Eddie "The Animal" Lopez was the undercard of the Thomas Hearns and Roberto Duran fight. It was one of the turning points in my boxing career. During that match, Lopez was relentless in boxing me. I would hit him with a five or six punch combination, but he would come back throwing punches! Amazingly, I won by a knock out in the 9th round. This fight changed the course of my career. It was the first time that Lopez had ever been knocked down! To put it in perspective, Eddie "The Animal" Lopez was more relentless in the ring against me than Mike Tyson who I would battle later.

From this point in my boxing career, after the Lopez match, I should have been booked for more competitive opponents. This was not the case again, however, due to my dad's poor management skills.

After my victory over "The Animal," I thought I was going to fight boxer Larry Holmes. I wanted to be super-prepared for this match. Mike Lagrone and I would get on our bikes and ride all around Detroit to different parks and playgrounds to train and build up my body for these challenging heavyweight fights. At the parks, we would crank out 200-500 push-ups, go all around the monkey bars for chin-ups and pull-ups, and from the ground do dips and sit-ups. We would do this from park to park. We would leave at 8:00 in the morning and not come back home until 8:00 that night. Yet, I never got to fight Larry Holmes, because my dad said that he would not take the fight, because they did not offer me enough money. Everyone saw that this was an unwise decision, even my future opponent, Mike Tyson.

Chapter 14- On the Road to the Championship

After winning string of fights, I was considered the number-one contender in the International Boxing Federation (IBF). At that time, Michael Spinks held that title, because he successfully defeated Larry Holmes, the previous title holder. In order for me to maintain being the number one contender, I had to fight James "Broad-Axe" Broad for the then vacant United States Boxing Association (USBA) Heavyweight title position. That fight took place at the Convention Hall in Atlantic City, New Jersey on August 26, 1986. After a grueling 12-round match, I successfully won by unanimous decision. I came into the ring with a record of 32 wins and 0 losses.

After my victory against James "Broad-Axe" Broad for the USBA Title, my dad thought that it would be best for us to leave the Kronk Gym camp in Michigan and move to Houston, Texas. In Houston, I trained with the heiress Josephine Abercrombie's camp. Josephine Abercrombie was one of the first female boxing promoters in history. I was in Houston, Texas at the Abercrombie camp with boxers like Frank Tate, an Olympic gold medalist, Hector "Macho" Camacho, Rodger Mayweather and Kevin Grove. Not to be outshined by my fellow boxers, the Houston training was punishing to stay in great shape for the ring.

Home Box Office (HBO) and Don King Productions put together a heavyweight unification series. They planned a match between me and the great Michael Spinks. We came to find out that for some reason or another Michael Spinks refused to fight me. He refused to defend his title against *me*. Keep in mind that I was the number-one contender for

Spinks's belt, the IBF Championship Title, the same one he had won from his victory over Larry Holmes. Eventually, given no other choice, the disappointed IBF withdrew, or literally *stripped*, its championship recognition of Michael Spinks on February 19, 1987. The International Boxing Federation said that the vacant title would be filled in an "immediate elimination series" between myself and the number-two contender, James "Buster" Douglas. The mandate was issued, and I was set to face Buster Douglas in the boxing ring.

Now during this period, there were in total three boxing sanctions (factions): the International Boxing Federation (IBF), the World Boxing Association (WBA), and the World Boxing Council (WBC). Each one of these groups had positioned to find the number-one contender in their respective sanction, rendering a representative for each. The idea behind it was to unify the titles into one champion altogether, so that one champion held all the belts.

When Michael Spinks refused to fight me and got stripped of his belt, the title should have gone directly to me without a match. After all, that's what happened when WBC declared Lennox Lewis the WBC Heavyweight Champion in December of 1992 after Riddick Bowe was stripped of his title. But this was not the plan for me. I went into the ring with James "Buster" Douglas, because he was the number-two contender, and I was the number-one contender. I knew that it was going to be a good, competitive fight, because I had sparred with Buster Douglas in the ring, and he was a *good* boxer. Prior to that fight, I had trained hard and was in top form for boxing.

On May 30, 1987 at the Las Vegas Hilton Outdoor Arena, I fought James "Buster" Douglas for the vacant International Boxing Federation belt. I came into the fight with a record of 34-0 with 29 knockouts. I was ready. My right hand was steady.

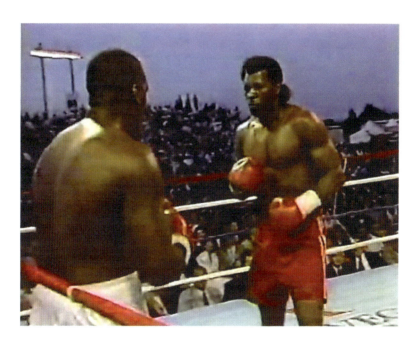

Do you see that look on my face in the photograph of me there in front of James "Buster" Douglas? It was Round 10, and I had Buster hurt. The only thing on my mind at that moment was my ultimate intention to finish him off. It was great boxing, and I won in the 10th round of a 15-round fight by a technical knockout and was declared the International Boxing Federation World Heavyweight Champion!

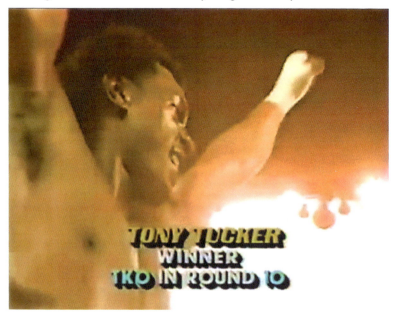

Chapter 15- Preparing for Mike Tyson

Victory was sweet but very short lived. I had the International Boxing Federation (IBF) title which I had just won by defeating Buster Douglas, and Mike Tyson had the World Boxing Council (WBC) and the World Boxing Association (WBA) titles. The pressure was on to immediately defend my title in a unification bout. We fought to unify the belts just 64 days, a mere two months after I had fought to win the IBF title. It did not give me any time to enjoy or process being a champion.

In that interim period prior to boxing Tyson, I was in the gym to seriously prepare for the upcoming fight. It was all about unifying the belts, and the powers at be would have it no other way. Back at the farm (the training camp) in Houston, I was getting ready for the fight against Mike Tyson and everything was going well. I was in very good shape.

Roger "The Black Mamba" Mayweather was one of the guys I would get to throw punches at me so I could practice ducking and dodging punches as a defensive tactic. If I could get out of the way of *this* guy, a lighter-weight who throws faster and a lot more punches than any heavyweight, then I knew I could get away from punches from someone who was much bigger and heavier. I also had Hector "Macho" Camacho throw punches at me, so I could master many other crucial boxing techniques.

It was down to two weeks before the grand match-up, our team arrived in Las Vegas. I was with some of my sparring partners for about 5 or 6 months, several of whom I got to know very well. They were on one accord with me winning the title. One sparring partner in particular had defeated Mike Tyson before in amateur boxing. But we did have one new guy who we called "Young Joe Lewis. "

"Young Joe Lewis" showed up at the gym and did a whole lot of mouthing off about what he was going to do to me: this, that, and the other- a real trash-talker. This matter was brought to my attention by one of my friends, a faithful sparring partner. Since this young man told everybody how much he was going to do me and because I had so many sparring partners, I decided that he would be my first sparring partner of the day. Understand that I would spar for 15 rounds. I would spar with some of my sparring partners for three rounds and with others for four rounds a-piece. So because Lewis was so verbal, I made him the first sparring partner I would put in the ring so that I could have the most energy to give him the most punishment out of all of my sparring partners.

I would stagger him in the ring, then I would let him get himself together, and I would stagger him again. This went on for a while during sparring practice until one time I hit him with my right hand, and I heard a soft pop and felt something peculiar under the glove. My heart dropped; I knew that it was something wrong. So I used my left hand for the remainder of the sparring.

When I returned to the corner for my one-minute break between rounds, I told my dad that I injured my right hand. He simply said to just go back out there and use my left hand. Well, *no kidding*! So, after the break, I went back in the ring and used my left hand. Just to check and see if my right hand was really hurt, I tried to use it again and found out that, indeed, my right hand was *seriously* hurt. I went back to the corner and informed my dad that there was something *seriously* wrong with my right hand. Roger Mayweather was there and witnessed that my right hand was really hurt.

After we confirmed that my right hand was badly injured, the commissioner doctor preformed an X-ray on my right hand. It was confirmed by the doctor that I had a hairline fracture in my right hand. After the doctor gave my dad and me the news about my hand, they left the room. After about several minutes, my dad and the doctor returned to the room where they left me waiting and the doctor informed me that after looking at my X-ray again, I would be able to continue boxing after 10 days of intensive therapy on my hand. This "intensive therapy" came in the form of specific instructions from the commissioner doctor for me to *not* to use my right hand, which happens to be my *good* right punch hand, for *10 straight days!* The fight was in 10 days!

Looking back, I should have known that there was no possibility that my right hand would have been healed in 10 days. Ultimately, the fight against Tyson should have been postponed until I was able to fight at my full potential. However, I, operating under what now I know was tunnel-vision, was focused only on the fight and did not really comprehend all that was happening surrounding the seriousness of my injury or the motives of the people around me. My injury came second to winning the fight. I had blinders on so much so that I was not even realizing that the doctor had just informed me that my right hand was broken; nor the fact that my father did not appear to understand the full scope of my injury and that my broken right hand could not be used in practice for 10 days. I just kept thinking it was going to be okay.

Chapter 16- The Tyson Fight

Like any son, I trusted and relied on my father, as both my manager and my parent, to make the right choice for me as a boxer and as his son. It is safe to say that I trusted that, after reviewing what the doctor had discussed, he would make the right decision for my career. I had no reason to second-guess that at all. I was thinking that by fight day, I would be ready, but that was not so. Regrettably, I found out that my loyalty to my father proved to be detrimental in more ways than one. Eventually, all of the seedy details began to unravel as how "Tucker," was dealing with his own personal issues and may not have made the best decisions regarding my boxing career. By all appearances and, although he was not the biblical depiction of Abraham, I was every bit his sacrificial lamb.

On August 1, 1987 in a Las Vegas Hilton, I, **Tony "TNT" Tucker** faced Mike Tyson. This would be the fight that would change the course of my life. It was the first time heavyweight contenders boxed for 12 rounds down from 15 rounds.

I remember the fight vividly, because I entered the ring with a broken right hand. Once inside the ring, I scooped Tyson up and hoisted him in the air with my left hand. Every time I used my right hand during that match I felt unbearable pain. This is when I realized that my hand was more than a simple fracture like the doctor mentioned. My hand was completely shot! This is when I realized that I would not be able to deliver my *"good night punch."* I was forced to use my left hand throughout most of the fight while using my right hand as a decoy. Amazingly, I was able to withstand a full twelve rounds with a damaged right hand against Tyson, who was never able to deliver a blow to hurt me during that fight.

The Tyson fight left me with three sharp jabs this time. The first one was that I was extremely disappointed in the loss I just suffered on national television for a shot at the heavyweight championship title. The second one was the fact that my father did not look out for my best interests for which I think all of this could have been avoided. And thirdly, I was going home with a severely broken hand.

In all actuality my dad should have been looking out for me. But that was not the case. The way I see it, the fight should have been postponed, but that was not the case either. I felt as if my father/manager should have been *the first* person who should have demanded that the fight be postponed. Overall, he should have made sure I went in the ring healthy, but unfortunately, that did not occur. Realizing all of the facts as they began to unfold and the fact that I should not have lost that fight made the jab of this hit feel as if it was a TKO. I knew that Mike Tyson was not supposed to beat me. He never even hurt me one time in that fight.

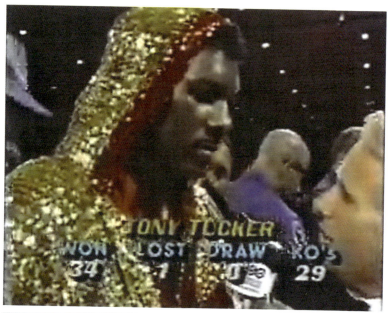

To add to the pain felt from what felt like a TKO was the aftermath of the fight. It is customary to give the post-fight interview, and I gave it; however, the facts associated with the match intensified the blow. I was forced to see Tyson on the television ads that were meant for me! That was supposed to be *my* Sprite commercial, for example. Losing that fight began to feel like mourning a death. It hurt to the core of my being. I had not experienced defeat in the ring for nine (9) years, and I was not mentally, psychologically or physiologically able to cope with it. When I walked out of the ring that night, it was if my whole body had taken several direct right punches without attempting to dodge them. It was the first time I really felt defeat, and it felt strange and foreign.

The next morning after the fight, I woke up thinking that I had just experienced a painful nightmare. However, once I rolled over and the pain began to set back in, I realized that I was still living in defeat. I couldn't seem to escape the loss. Everywhere I went, even in my despondent state of mind, people recognized me. Although I had loss against Tyson, the fight itself gave me more notoriety than ever before. People began to know and see me as "the boxer who Mike Tyson was not able to knock out" and "the boxer who fought Mike Tyson with one hand for twelve rounds." While in my pity, I had not been thinking of myself in terms of the success I had accomplished in the fight; the only thing I focused on was the fact that Tyson was not supposed to beat me.

It was not long after that short-lived fame that I realized I was robbed of all my money. As a boxer, I had been "sold out" by so many people, especially those whom I trusted. The people I trusted most were the ones who deceived me both inside and outside of the ring. I was revealed to be the proverbial sacrificial lamb, and that was a blow to my gut. My dad, whom I loved and trusted, was not always forthright in the decisions that he made in guiding my boxing career. My father was street smart, but he was not able to withstand all the crooks out there used to ripping others off for a living. Nor could he fight the drug demons that ensnared him.

Chapter 17- The Pretty White Devil

After the Mike Tyson fight, I felt as if I had been knocked out of life altogether. It felt as if I would never regain consciousness. I had reconciled in my mind that the only cure for my constant state of delirium could only be found in the streets. Having been sorely disappointed and mad at my dad, I ventured to the streets in search for something, anything, that would ease the pain I felt.

While on my quest to find relief for my constant pain, I began to attend many Hollywood star-studded parties located in luxurious mansions as a temporary anesthetic. I remember attending one party in particular in Beverly Hills. Even though I was at one of my lowest points, I still felt in the mix with all of these big entertainers by having what I felt like was exclusive access to these "top-notch" affairs. While at the party, I would see different men and women, most of which were celebrities, entering and exiting out of the various rooms of the mansion, and I wondered what could be going down behind those closed doors. Still perplexed as to what was all going on in the mysterious rooms, I remained in awe, because it was a lot of people that I recognized from television.

As the party continued and I continued to take in all that was going on around me, I noticed from a distance a woman pointing towards me and telling me to come over to her. I looked around and thought she was pointing to someone else. But as she continued to stare in my direction and keep her finger fixated at the center of my chest, I realized that she *was* pointing to *me*, **Tony "TNT" Tucker**, and that she was asking me to come over to her. "Hmmm", I thought to myself, "Maybe I would be able to get behind one of those mysterious closed doors other celebrities so frequently entered and exited." I wasn't about to pass up the offer, and I didn't.

Eventually I eased off the leather couch where I sat and made my way across the room to where she waited for me. With long legs and a curvaceous body, she was very seductive and attractive. I thought I hit the jackpot! As we finally entered the room, she began to tell me how she was able to turn powdered cocaine into a hard substance. Too struck by her beauty, I was unaware of the fact that she was giving me an actual scientific lesson on freebasing. Prior to entering that room, I had never touched drugs. I was an athlete and I prided myself in keeping clean and in good physical condition. It was a discipline that I practiced religiously throughout my life. I had been exposed to powder but never crack or free basing. All of this was a new arena for me.

As the night went on, I never caught this woman's name. The only thing I remember about the mysterious, alluring woman was that she showed me how to smoke cocaine. I remember her breaking off a piece of the rock with her long finger nails and placing it, ever so gently, as if it were a precious jewel, inside the pipe. Then she demonstrated how to get high. She made it look irresistible. I immediately followed her instructions so that I could smoke it exactly the way she did.

I hit that pipe hard! As I was taking all of that crack pipe into my mouth, she kneeled down, reached down into my pants and began to take all of my pipe into her mouth. Before I knew it, I was smoking crack and a beautiful woman was performing oral sex on me. As I blew out smoke from my head from the crack pipe, I felt the urge to release from my head below. The feeling of both simultaneously was overwhelming. As the oral sex intensified, I had the most intense orgasm! This feeling, along with my first high was indescribable. For the first time in weeks, I have felt alive. The pain I felt from losing the Tyson fight and all of my money was suddenly diminished. Smoking cocaine became the remedy to my pain. It would later turn into an addiction that would be the source of great pain and suffering. It was the *white devil.*

Chapter 18- Downward Descent

After that initial high at that party in Beverly Hills, I began a downward spiral that would last for far too many years and cost me more than I could have ever imagined. There is a very high cost associated with low living. That price was not just monetarily. I would eventually pay in relationships, in friends, and in major damage to families. Aside from your own health, your family is the first one affected by drug addiction.

Soon, I found myself in all kinds of places that many people only see in Hollywood movies. I was in hotels and motels and wherever I could escape to get high. One of the side effects of getting high off crack cocaine was to suffer extreme paranoia. An example of which was described at the opening of this book when I shared my situation with you about the Rodney King riots in Los Angeles.

I started getting high at the time that crack cocaine was making its way into mainstream America. After I became part of this crowd, many dark days lay ahead for me on a twisted path. Following the Tyson fight, I had to disconnect from my father, the only person in my life for many years whom I believed knew anything about the boxing game despite his managerial shortcomings. His deceit, his lies, and the robbery were all too much for me to handle. Little did I know, my dad was on his own personal addiction mission, and crack had him in its grip as well. Like I said before, my dad was a super-genius in the *art* of Boxing, but he did not know the *business* of Boxing. My dad trained Floyd Mayweather, Sr. who went on to start Roger Mayweather into boxing. Floyd, Sr. later trained his son, Floyd Mayweather, Jr. All of them are the fruit of the labor of my father, Robert Tucker. In the end, my superhero evolved into to be my greatest disappointment.

Ever since that initial experience at the party in Beverly Hills, nothing in my life seemed to go right. I ended up reconnecting with that same female who introduced me to the drugs and found out that she was *a carrier*. A carrier was a person who holds drugs for big dealers. She *always* had drugs. So I hooked up with her again, because she was the only person that I knew who could supply me with that feeling that she gave me initially. We got high together on a regular basis.

My cousin Jamie (James Childrey) could not stand her! He knew she was the devil, and he helplessly watched my demise. There was not anything he or anyone else could do for me as I chased that ever-elusive high. Later, my brother, Donnie, came out to Las Vegas. He was aware of my newfound addiction to drugs, and he could not stand me because of it, either. Since Donnie usually looked up to me, my behavior hurt him deeply. I was once his protector, but now, I couldn't even protect myself from myself.

Chapter 19- Functioning Addict

Most people think that once you start getting high, you cannot function nor do anything else in life. But there are many functioning addicts and alcoholics out there. They are the most dangerous in a sense, because they can keep the addiction hidden and are less likely to believe they have a problem. I was one of these people.

While on crack, I continued to box. I would go away to training camp, and in that training environment, I did not get high. Training every day with people around me constantly, I *could* not get high. Also, the need to get high diminished, because I was back doing what I loved. Training for the ring temporarily replaced the desire to get high. However, right after any fight, regardless if I emerged victorious or not, what I can only describe as a dark cloud would come over me and engulf my very being. That cloud would be accompanied by this terrible feeling of boredom and an insatiable craving for that release. It was brutal.

Eventually, I would return to the underworld, seeking the white devil. The only accurate description that I can give is that I was being driven by demons. That is the only way I can describe the darkness that surrounded me at that time. It was a deep, dark desire and craving that was never fulfilled.

Like many addicts have explained, you never get that feeling that you had the first time. You are always chasing that very first high! It is never fulfilled, but you just keep on chasing it. When I was in the ring, I would get a high from the audience and all of the accolades. When I was not smoking and back in the ring, my presence there would temporarily feel the void. Boxing would feed the ego, but crack would feed my spirit. It was a vicious cycle. Out of all of the years that I did drugs, I never felt that initial feeling that I had when I first smoked at that Beverly Hills party. It was a constant and brutal chase. The craving that you have for crack outweighs any and every sensibility that you have or should possess. It seemed more important than eating food or drinking water; however, it was never a time when crack became more important in my life than boxing *so long as I had opportunities to box*. As long as I was in a training camp, my addiction was controlled. If I knew I was getting ready for a fight, I knew I had to be ready and get right. Preparing to box set me on a path that was more important than getting high, at least temporarily. I always tried to quit: Over and over and over again…

Chapter 20- You Quit a Thousand Times

You quit a thousand times before you really quit! There were a few times during my career that I went to rehab, two rehabs to be exact. Both stints in rehab were epic failures. The reason they were unsuccessful was because I would quit for a period of time but would always return to the white devil's pipe. Both times my desire to stay clean was very short-lived. The lure was too much, and both times I found myself back doing what I despised. I had no control over my life, even less control than when I let others manage it.

After the honors and celebrity had diminished, I was left to myself, surrounded by a dark cloud of boredom. As the shadows crept in, the insatiable craving engulfed me, forcing me back to the pipe again. It was a vicious cycle. I realized during the course of writing this book that I suffered from two addictions: the first to celebrity and the second to crack cocaine. The only thing I can compare it to was like the rush I felt getting in the boxing ring in front of a massive audience. It also was comparable in danger where one wrong punch could be fatal. Now, I trained to be in the ring with other boxers, so it must have been divine intervention that I was able to duck, dodge, and roll punches in the ring with crack.

The truest statement I could make regarding addiction at the lowest level is that you find yourself in the depths of despair, a deep, dark hole. I quit a thousand times. I would always declare, "This is it, I am never going back," only to go back again. I would ask the Lord to forgive me each time, but I would go back again. I was powerless against crack cocaine and held for ransom by a drug that had me bound in its grips. The required payment was my very own freedom and my dignity.

It was not until I was truly tired, fed up with myself and really wanted to quit that hope came my way. I had so many suspended drivers' licenses and numerous drinking and driving citations. I never got caught with the crack on me, but I was found with crack paraphernalia. Even after all of this, I would always claim I was ready to let it go.

One night after making a drug run, I was driving back home and ran head-on into a lady in a van. I saw the look of panic and terror on her face. I got out of my car and went over to her vehicle and asked if she was okay. She was pretty much in shock that I had ran into her car, but she appeared to be alright, so I got back in my car and proceeded to go home. I needed to get high. It was a hit and run, but I didn't care. A few days later, the police tracked me and my wrecked automobile down, and I had to deal with the consequences of that incident.

Still, the only thing that was on my mind was getting high. That craving outweighs all sensibility.

Chapter 21- The First Payment

During the two-year time span after I fought Mike Tyson, I spent a lot time with Channel, the mother of my oldest daughter, Francesca. We traveled between Las Vegas and New York while I struggled with my drug addiction. I no longer had a solid footing with boxing career, because my relationship with my dad was strained. My boxing career was in limbo, because I did not know where to go or what to do without my dad's direction, even for the little things. Once, my loyalty to him was unquestionable, but I knew that I could not let him manage me again due to all the ignorance, manipulation and greed that took place during the first part of my career. My dad was on drugs at the time as well and fighting his own demons.

I was just all out, addicted to drugs. There just simply was no one else for me to turn to for guidance. The only thing I knew on my own about boxing was how to get in the ring and box. Finally, I reconnected with Shelly Finkel and Gary Gittlesohn who advised me to go rehab. They were going to start managing my career. I complied and entered rehab in upstate New York.

Rehab opened me up so that I could start thinking again. It was exactly what I needed at the time, and it went very well. I didn't have access to any drugs. I needed a break from the drugs. My brain was shut down from drug usage. I was housed in a very nice place in New York City and life was good. It seemed perfect to me. I felt alive again. During this time, I was training and going to the gym every day and going to the daily Narcotics Anonymous (NA) meetings in order to get ready for the ring.

One day, I was leaving the gym heading back home, after I stopped and picked up a card and balloon for Channel for Valentine's Day. I saw this young lady, and she asked me about the balloons. I told her that I purchased them for my girlfriend and was on my way to see her. The young lady commented on that being a nice gesture and then gave me a card inviting me and Channel to a party they were having that evening. She told me that, if I had a chance, I should just stop by. The conversation ended and I headed home. When I finally arrived home, Channel was there waiting for me. I presented her the balloons and the card for Valentine's Day. She did not want to go out anywhere, so we just relaxed at home for a bit. After a while, I got bored and the thought was in the back of my mind about the party that we had been invited to earlier. I told Channel that I was going out for a while and I went to the party. Little did I know, the devil was waiting for me at that party.

    I walked in the door. And what I saw was everything I feared but knew was going to be there anyway: the drugs, the pipe, the scenery. It was all so irresistibly there, and I fell right back into it like a ton of bricks. I had been clean for a while. Now, here I was, back to square one. I was off and running again. The chase was once again on for that elusive high.

    Initially, I started hiding my usage. But this time, Channel knew right off when she saw me. She left me right there by myself in the middle of New York City. I eventually kept going right back to the same place where I attended that party. I was back in the underworld again and it would be hell to get out.

    Back in the boxing world, my trainer was the first to find out about my drug usage. He then reported my relapse to my manager. As soon as it was exposed, they quickly shipped me to Tucson, Arizona, to another rehab.

    At this particular rehab center, I ran into some NFL players and rock stars who also were suffering with addiction. Everything was going along well at this center. I had been in treatment for about 35 days and they suggested that I stay two more weeks because they said I was not ready to be discharged yet. However, I refused to stay there two more weeks, because I was missing Channel, and I felt that I was clean and free from drugs. I checked myself out and left against their admonitions for me to stay for two more weeks.

I left that rehab in Arizona and headed back to New York City, and instead of them giving me my own place this time, they housed me with a trainer at his house with his family. Everything was going along fine. I was back in the gym training every day and getting back into good shape. Shelly and Gary were working to get me clean and back in the ring. I did not have any fights set up or anything at that time. They were two people who truly had my best interest at heart.

One weekend, they let me use a car and go see Channel. After my visit with her, I went back down to the drug hole. I ventured to the same location of the Valentine's party several months ago. As a result, I did not make it back to my trainer's house for 3 or 4 days. I crashed from a cocaine coma, a white sleep, and the people at the drug house told me that while I was crashed out, they had taken my trainer's car to make a drug run. Since I was awake, they gave me some more drugs, and I was off and running again. It was indeed a vicious cycle.

After that incident, as it was the third time that I failed, Shelly called me into his office and had *the talk*. He told me that I was never going to make it. He told me that I was never going to be champion and that my career was over. They handed me a plane ticket and shipped me back home to Las Vegas.

When I returned to Vegas, I checked out my house and my Benz to make sure everything was good. Then, I went back out on the chase again. I came across a drug dealer who ended up becoming a friend and living with me. Low-level living drove me to the streets with a television for sale. I saw this dude coming down the street and asked him if he wanted to buy the TV (with my intent to score crack). He said that he was more interested in *my Benz*. So I said to him, "Let me show you something," and I put him in my Benz and drove him to my mini mansion. The dealer complimented me on my house, but said that it just needed to be cleaned up. It was a filthy mess! Housekeeping is not a priority when you are trying to get high. He brought a crew of girls over and they cleaned up my place, and I offered him a room in my house. I had drugs all the time and girls on demand, at my fingertips. In my delusional mindset I was the man.

Chapter 22- Boxing During my Dark Days

Nearly two years after the Mike Tyson fight, I got back in the ring and I had a string of victories under my belt including the fight against Orlin Norris. Stacey McKinley was my trainer and Jack Cohen managed me at that time.

Orlin Norris was the reigning North American Boxing Federation (NABF) Heavyweight Champion. My match against him was for the title. The fight was held on June 3, 1991 at Caesar's Palace in Las Vegas.

TALE OF THE TAPE

	TONY TUCKER		ORLIN NORRIS
HEIGHT	6'5"		5'9"
WEIGHT	235		213
AGE	32		25
REACH	81½		70

After being away from the ring so long and being shrouded in darkness, I was still able to defeat Orlin Norris and win the NABF Heavyweight Champion title. However, my victory was short-lived because I was still riding the roller coaster of drug addiction, the one where you want to jump up while going downhill, but the continuous craving drives you to go after that ever-elusive high.

My dad would stop by my house occasionally to see how I was doing and what was going in my life. I was way out there beyond anyone's reach, thrusted into the depths of darkness and despair. One day my dad stopped by to tell me about some guy in California who wanted to introduce himself to me. My dad suggested that I get myself together and get clean so that the guy could come out to Las Vegas to meet with me. The man's name was Edmond Bell. After meeting with Mr. Bell, it wasn't long before I was moving to Big Oaks, located in the California mountains. Once in California, I was back to training at one of the better training camps I had ever entered.

A guy named "Big John" ran the camp. There was a road next to the property that we dubbed "Pain Lovers Road" because of its steep incline. This road was excellent for training. I would do 5 miles up and 5 miles down this road daily. I was on my way to getting back in the boxing ring again.

A month before my first fight, I had Channel and my daughter come down and go to Disney Land. We were considering getting back together, and things were going well. We had a blast spending time together, but they soon returned home. Later, I had them come back for the fight, so that Channel could see that I was off of drugs and back in the ring again.

My next fight was against Dino Homsey. I defeated Homsey with a solid knockout. Everything was uphill from that point. I had a clean streak for a very long time. During which, I also fought and defeated Mike Rouse in Seattle, Washington. Things were going great, and I stayed in California and fought at the Great Western Forum. My life was back on track.

During my travels, I met a nice young lady named Kim Jackson. We went on a date to Magic Mountain and I suggested that she stay over at a hotel instead of taking the long drive home to Los Angeles. At the hotel, I asked Kim for her keys and took her car into Los Angeles for my own purposes. I drove straight into the underworld again, where I stayed all night. I did not come back to the hotel until the next morning.

When I arrived back at the hotel, Kim was real sweet about what I did. She did not lash out at me or scold me or any of the things that one would expect from a woman who was left alone in a hotel room all night. I told her the truth about what I did in Los Angeles: that I got high and ended up staying there all night with her car. She accepted that truth, and we moved on with our relationship.

Kim worked for the airline and every weekend she would fly back home with the expectation of seeing me. She was perfectly fine with me getting high. Even with her in my life, I was still given to get high. Eventually, I married Kim, feeling that she was someone of understanding and support. During this time I finally severed all business ties with my dad due to the constant mishandling of finances. Between severing ties with my dad and Kim's acceptance, my drug use escalated.

Back at the training camp, I prepared for my fight against Lionel Washington for the USA California State Heavyweight Title. Stacey McKinley and Jack Cohen were still my trainer and manager. I would always stop getting high so that I could train. When my dad was my manager getting high was not an issue, because he, in fact was getting high as well. When I was fighting consistently, I would stay clean for a while and then fall off again. It was the roller coaster ride of drug addiction.

In between the time that I fought Orlin Norris and Kimmuel Odum I signed with Don King. The year was 1992, and I was on a winning streak. I had to defend my NABF Heavyweight title against challenger Oliver McCall at the Cleveland State Convocation Centre in Cleveland, Ohio on June 26, 1992. It was a challenging match but I won the fight against Oliver McCall in a split-decision and held on to the NABF Heavyweight title and finished out the year with a slate of wins.

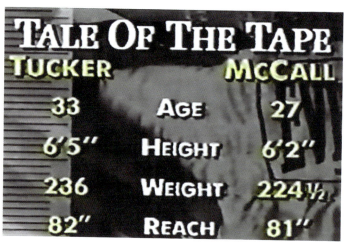

Chapter 23- Lennox Lewis Handicap Match

The next big fight for me was the bout against Lennox Lewis. In the midst of everything that was going on in my personal life outside of the ring, including my drug addiction, I was presented with another opportunity for the WBC Heavyweight title. I was ranked number one by the WBC. Lennox Lewis was the first British-born boxer to hold a world heavyweight title since Bob Fitzsimmons in 1897.

There was a crowd of about 15,000 people at the Thomas & Mack Center in Las Vegas, Nevada. This photo of me draped in the flag was representative of me boxing to represent the USA as Lennox boxed to represent Great Britain.

I went into the ring to fight Lennox Lewis as a 34-year-old professional boxer with a record of 48-1-1. However, I was not at the top of my game. I could no longer box at 100% because of the white devil, the use of crack cocaine. It was the first time in my boxing career that I was knocked off my feet. I was knocked down in the 3rd round and again in the 9th round. His right hand caught me and landed a huge blow. If you watch the match, you will see that I was not utilizing one of the main strategies I learned early on in my career: roll with the punches. I had lost my edge and was not rolling with the punches at all. My use of drugs outside of the ring took away some of my fight inside the ring.

I would always quit getting high to prepare for the ring, but the body can only take so much abuse. The roller coaster of ups and downs and highs and lows took its toll on my body. I lost both my stamina and my drive. Drugs stripped me of my strength. Like Samson from the Bible, my strength was gone, but I was not aware of it at all. I went out to box like Samson with no hair, unaware that I no longer had the edge. It was indeed a sad state of affairs. Thinking that I could smoke crack cocaine while I was not boxing, stop to train and box, and then go back to smoking crack was foolish. I was fooling myself. Self-deception was at its highest level, and self-deception is the absolute worst deception.

Lennox Lewis deservingly won in a unanimous 12-round decision. But he didn't know he had an unknown, unwanted, invisible partner at his side: my white devil. It was really 2-on-1; in professional wrestling, they call this a handicap match. This fight was much different from the Tyson fight. I was not physically injured, and my father was not in the picture. This was all Tony "TNT" Tucker living and boxing in the arena of self-deception: smug, arrogant, and ignorant.

Chapter 24- The Fallout

After Lennox Lewis fight, my contract with Don King's expired. Jack Cohen remained my manager. For the remainder of that year, I managed to fight and win a string of bouts in the U.S. and Mexico.

In the meantime George Foreman refused to defend his WBA World Heavyweight title against me, choosing to fight Axel Schulz instead. This decision positioned me to fight against Bruce Seldon for the vacant WBA belt in April 1995.

I was a fan favorite. I came into the ring with a record of 52-2-1 including 43 knockouts. My trainer was George E. Paige. It felt good to be back at Caesar's Palace. This was my second chance for a world title. Although my lifestyle had not changed outside of the ring, my discipline remained the same: stopping drugs only to train for boxing.

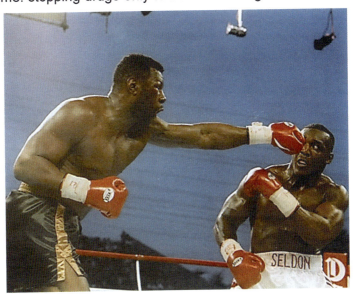

Bruce Seldon delivered some big blows in that fight, one of which landed me on the eye. That quick blow ended up damaging my eye. The doctors on site conferred with officials and the fight was stopped in Round 7. This was a first for me. I was shocked because I felt as if I was able to continue boxing, but it was not to be. The attending physician made the call to stop the fight for safety reasons.

This period of my life continued to be some of the darkest days for me, both inside and outside of the ring. Not only was I still in the grips of the white devil, crack cocaine, I was married to a woman who suffered with a severe gambling addiction.

I would repeat the same cycle when it came to prepare for a fight: stop using, train, box and use again. After each fight, whether I won or loss, that white devil would be there relentlessly. That demon that had possessed me for so long, would continuously beckon me into its dwelling as if I was the only person able to occupy it. You see, once you hit that crack pipe, its game over. You ultimately almost become a permanent resident in the house of the devil, a place no person truly desires to be.

Chapter 25- Still Taking its Toll

After the Seldon match, I suffered a string of losses. This was the first time I had experienced this in my boxing career. I began to wallow in the depths of despair. There seemed to be no escape from the strong clutches of the white devil, as my descent into the depths of hell became more dark and tormented.

I knew I would never get another opportunity for a rematch against Seldon for the title when later that year I lost to Don King's newly signed boxer Henry Akinwande by a unanimous decision. The following year, I was back in the ring with old rival Orlin Norris at the Richmond Coliseum in Richmond, Virginia, where I suffered another loss.

Boxing was all that I knew. I was groomed to be a boxer since I was a little boy. I had never entertained the thought of doing anything else once I decided to be a boxer nor had I envisioned any type of life outside of the ring.

As fate would have it, another opportunity presented itself in the ring for the vacant NABF Heavyweight title. The title had been vacated by Alexander Zolkin in order to fight Henry Akinwande for the WBO title. At the age of 37, I came into the ring at the Fantasy Springs Casino, in Indio, California, with a record of 52-5- 1 with 43 knockouts. My fight was against David Dixon in the 123-degree California desert heat. The fight was over in the 1st round. It was a gross mismatch, but nevertheless I was in possession of the NABF Heavyweight title. I had redeemed myself, at least in my own mind, from the previous three losses.

My life outside the ring was not one of interviews and endorsements as one may think a boxer of my caliber would have. Personally, I did not have any products of my own or anything that would represent any other source of income outside of boxing. To add insult to injury, the income that was coming in quickly depleted, given my drug addiction and my wife's gambling habits.

When I was fighting consistently, I did not run out of money; therefore I did not run out of rocks (crack cocaine). It was relatively easy to feed my addiction and finance my wife's gambling addiction. However, when you run out of money you run out of rocks, and that in and of itself became extremely problematic.

Meanwhile, while still struggling with my addiction, the stage was being set for another shot at the WBO title. This fight was set up by Don King. During these final title fights, instead of the matches focusing on me, my name was used to build other fighters. Nevertheless, it was an opportunity to fight Herbie Hide for the vacant WBO title. On the flip side, I was in very bad shape. I was still living in the height of self-deception: riding the rollercoaster of addiction's ups and downs, highs and lows, and ins and outs. I still had enough resolve to maintain the cycle.

The fight against Dixon left me somewhat delusional. I won the fight and believed that I was back on top of my game. But that certainly was not the case in reality. Years of drug abuse gradually took its toll on my body and mind. It became more and more evident in the ring.

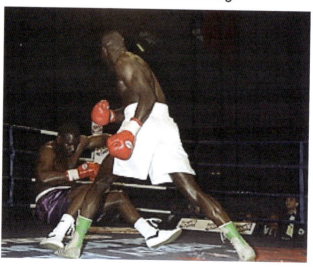

For example, the match against Herbie Hide, for the first time in my illustrious boxing career, I was knocked out. "***Tony 'TNT' Tucker* Knocked out by Herbie Hide,**" was the headline. It was painful to endure, but not painful enough to make me stop living the lie I was living outside of the ring. It was not painful enough for me to stop smoking crack cocaine. The use of drugs dulls all sensitivity to a normal life. Nothing about my life was normal, but the white devil made that seem okay. I was a World Heavyweight Boxing Champion addicted to crack cocaine. That *was* my reality.

I was in the bondage of drug addiction, still trying to box, and being used by everyone and anyone who could use me. I have learned that if you do not know who you are, people will use you or make you into anyone they want you to be. In my altered state of mind, I did not realize that I had lost who I really was a long time ago. In my mind, I could keep boxing forever. Little did I know, my career was coming to an abrupt end.

Chapter 26- Counting the Costs

During my marriage to Kim, she was tasked with taking care of our taxes and things related to finances in our household. But something went wrong. The IRS came in and hit all of our bank accounts and cleaned them out in one stroke. Every single penny was gone. My wife, the gambling addict, never saw to it that our taxes were paid. It was a nightmare unfolding in front of my very eyes. You would think I would have learned from being burned by my father not to entrust my finances to anyone else. Obviously, that was not the case. I again entrusted my money to someone close to me, someone I should have been able to trust, my wife. After this, whenever I had a fight, the IRS was at the box office to get my money. To say the least, it was a very humbling and depressing experience.

In the lowest levels of my drug addiction there were times when I would be out of cash and craving crack cocaine in the worst way. At that time, I owned a sexy blue Mercedes. I would make my way over to the "hood" in Las Vegas where I knew I could score some rocks. When I pulled up, I would let the window down in my car and call one of the dope boys over to my car and ask him to show me his product. They knew who I was and thought that I was about to make a big purchase, which I normally did when the money was flowing. Gladly, the dope dealer would stick a handful of rocks through my window for me to examine. I would then smack them out of his hand so that the rocks could land on the floor of my car, and I would speed off, leaving him empty handed and pissed. I was desperate to get high. I headed back to my mini mansion where I would be posted up in my master bedroom, and I would smoke myself into oblivion.

I would repeat that same scenario on a few other occasions, except I would lure the dope boy with a wad of money. I would have one large denomination wrapped over a lot of one-dollar bills or paper or whatever the case may be, and I would ask him to show me some rocks, at which time I would do the same scam.

The number of times I would find myself passed out from a cocaine coma or just lost in time are too numerous to mention. There is no sense of time, urgency, responsibility, or life. Drugs have absolutely no respect for time. While you are on drugs, 5 or 10 years could have gone by and you never would realize it is gone. Drugs eat up time. The only thing on your mind in the depths of addiction is getting high. Who I was and what I had accomplished never came into play.

Like I said, drugs have no regard for life. There was a time I went to purchase drugs and had a gun pointed at my temple. If it had not been for the grace of God, I would have been shot at point blank-range. Often, I would attempt to disguise myself to venture into the places where I would purchase drugs. However, I was always recognized. I remember one occasion where a guy said to me, "Aren't you Tony 'TNT' Tucker?" He said, "I know you, man. You are a big-time boxer". I acknowledged who I was and went on to purchase some rocks, not caring about the potential exposure of my addiction.

Drug addiction affects everybody else around you, including your family. Once, I was home visiting my mom, and she pleaded for me to stop getting high. My addiction hurt her deeply. Unmoved, I remember leaving the house to go get high, and her chasing after me. I was still in pretty good shape and just took off running past her, but she still kept pursuing. Then, I thought to myself that she was going to have a heart attack trying to keep up with me, so I stopped running as to not kill my mom. My mother loved me unconditionally then and still does to this very day. She has always been there for me no matter what condition, situation or circumstance I found myself. There is no love like a mother's love, but even that was not enough to make me quit; her love, in and of itself, was powerless against my drug addiction.

Chapter 27- The End of It All

Again, my name was used for title fights to build the names of other fighters. My father found himself back in position as my trainer. At 39 years old with a record of 56-6-1 and 43 knockouts, I found myself at the Ice Palace in Tampa, Florida challenging John Ruiz for the NABF title. Before the end of the 1st round, I was laid out on the canvass for the 4th time in my boxing career. Realistically, my drug-addicted mind could not pull off a victory. There was a huge disconnect between my mind and my body. Having sustained years of drug addiction I was barely able perform the one thing that was second nature to me. For my age and condition, I mustarded, as evidenced in the 6th round, but this fight would prove to be the beginning of the end of my career.

Just like a rollercoaster, an incline comes before the dramatic drop. After a few months, I was back in the ring to fight against Billy Wright. It was at Sam's Town Casino, Tunica, Mississippi, which was a long way from the big Las Vegas fights that I was used to. The fight lasted all of one round. I managed to knock out Billy Wright in the first round.

After the Billy Wright fight, I was scheduled to fight in Vegas at the Las Vegas Hilton. The prospect of getting back to Vegas to fight was exciting. During the physical, the doctors detected that I had a detached retina, and they would not allow me to fight. Hearing that news tore me up. I was not ready to quit boxing. *It could not just end like this.* After all, this is what I did for my entire life. Ultimately, I did not retire by choice; I was retired by force like a dry marker.

The day that I was retired was the same day that my wife walked out on me. Without my income or fame to support her, she was gone and then filed for divorce. I was emotionally shot. Inside, I felt dead. My career was over before I even realized it and I did not have any choice in the matter. Furthermore, I was gripped by fear. I had nothing else lined up. *Nothing.* All I had ever known was boxing. Now I didn't even have a wife to comfort me.

At this point I went full throttle into the arms of the white devil. I started using every single day. To say that I was deeply depressed would be an understatement. Eventually, I lost my Mercedes Benz. My car was paid for, but I was in an accident and damaged my hood. I put my Benz in the body shop for repairs, but I did not have enough money to get it out. They sold my Benz to recover the cost of the repairs.

Finally, I could not keep up with the mortgage on my house so I lost that, too. During my marriage, as I have stated previously, my wife had a gambling habit and I had a drug addiction. I could have paid my house off many times over, but because of spending so much on my drug addiction and her gambling addiction, that never happened. In the end, I felt kind of relieved not having the pressure of a mortgage because the IRS was set to take it away anyway. Bills, mortgages, and issues related to everyday family living were not priorities.

After I lost my house, my mom came to Las Vegas and helped me move into an apartment. This was one of the darkest times of my life. I also had a friend, Jerry, who helped from time to time with getting drugs and helped me to get along with bills and that sort of thing. I was reduced to working security at the apartment complex. *Tony "TNT" Tucker, former World Heavyweight Boxing Champion was working security at an apartment complex.* It was an humbling experience and really not all that bad. I did not have the pressure to prepare for fights or the concern of high living expenses.

I had no transportation after losing my car, so I had to ride the bus. Actually, I had to *learn* how to ride the bus as I had never ridden a bus before. This was a foreign concept. The good part was that the supermarket that I went to was not far, so I would walk there and take one of their carts and walk back home with my groceries.

My eye was severely damaged, but I was in denial about it. But things worked out, and I had surgery on my eye; however, since I had gone too long without treatment, my eye was permanently damaged.

After staying at the complex for a couple of years, I met Tracy, the sister of one of my crack partners. She did not smoke crack or do anything related to drug use. It was not a romantic relationship at all; it was just a friendship with a really down-to-earth person. She would come and spend time with me and take me back to her place for the weekends. Eventually, I ended up moving in with Tracy and left Jerry at my apartment. While I was away, Jerry burned my apartment down. That was problematic, because I figured that if things did not work out with me and Tracy living together I would have a place to go back to, but Jerry burned it down. Then I found myself in the precarious position of having to live with Tracy. But then *her* place got burned down. Could it get any worse? I had no job and I was still in love with my ex-wife.

Chapter 28- Exit Orders

During this time of limbo and transition, I picked up a job at a local nightclub. It did not pay much of anything. However, it was while I was working at the club that I met some people from Tampa, Florida. One of the guys knew of my boxing fame and told me that if I came to Florida, they would help me out and introduce me to one of their partners. I pondered over the scenario for a while, but what really helped me make the decision to move was an incident that happened.

One day, I was coming out of a cocaine coma, and I sensed someone standing over me. At first, I could not quite figure out the voice, for I was very groggy. I did not open my eyes, but I heard the person standing over me say that she just ought to just stab me right then and there, and she named another person she intended to stab as well. I laid there for a while and pretended to be sleep, but I knew I had to get out of the situation. The person who was standing over me was Tracy. Needless to say, that particular incident was my exit order. She was a nutcase, and I was not about to stick around and be killed by a psychotic woman with whom I only had a platonic relationship.

Eventually, Lewis called me and sent me a ticket to come to Florida. I was more than happy to escape the situation I found myself in at that time. They took me to a nightclub in Tampa and set up housing for me in the southern part of the city. Things were going along very well, and I met some other people and started working in a local nightclub to generate some income. One of the key persons that I met when I arrived in Florida was Carlo. As fate would have it, he was then and still remains a good friend, supporter and confidante. He has been there with me through the good, the bad and the ugly.

Nothing had changed in terms of my relationship with the white demon except for the fact that I had started drinking more alcohol than ever. It was a lethal combination: drugs *and* alcohol. While working at the nightclub, I was getting high, drinking and driving. My addictions were completely out of control at this point. I was a train wreck and a "walking dead" in the making.

Chapter 29- A Light in the Darkness

I am very grateful to a pastor named Robert Johnson. He used to pray for me and come rescue me from the hotels. Pastor Johnson would even call me sometimes and just pray for me over the phone. Most times, I would see it was him on the caller ID and not answer, but he would leave me a voicemail message. Pastor Johnson would encourage me to get up from that place and he would simply motivate me. I had no transportation, so when I needed a ride, I would call Pastor Johnson; he would come and pick me up from wherever I was holed up. Most importantly, when he prayed for me, he would anoint me with oil and then drop me off at home.

Pastor Johnson was never judgmental or condescending; rather, he was always uplifting and encouraging. He was my angel in disguise and a true blessing to me in those days. It was the combination of his prayers and the prayers of many others that kept me in those darkest of days. Ultimately, it would be me personally applying this method of prayer for myself that would lead to the defeat of the white demon.

These were very dark and disparaging days. Like I mentioned before, back when I was fighting, I did not run out of money, so I did not run out of rocks. But when I ran out of money and ran out of rocks, it became a serious problem at the end of my drug addiction journey. I look back over it, now; and I cannot tell you what drove me to such depths of despair. The combination of drugs and alcohol broke my spirit and stole my will. They rendered me totally and completely useless and void of life.

Chapter 30- Back at it Again

Famed boxing trainer Angelo Dundee lived in the Florida area at the time when I finished drug court. It was him who actually presented me with my certificate of graduation from drug court. Angelo was very encouraging to me during that time. He came to be the person who presented me with my certificate due to the wisdom and insight of a judge who worked at the court. She must have known what it would mean to me and arranged for this to happen. I was very appreciative, because she went out of her way to make this happen.

Following my graduation of drug court, I once again decided that I was going to fight the white demon again and not use cocaine anymore. So I switched my addiction focus from smoking cocaine to drinking; I decided to stop smoking and just drink instead. The plan to drink in the place of drugs worked for a little while until one day when I got so drunk, I ended up right back in the drug-hole underworld. It was, AGAIN, back to the vicious cycle of chasing that elusive high all over again. Addiction is an unrelenting bitch. I wish I could find some other word to describe it, but right now that is the only thing that comes to mind.

When working at the nightclub, I would drink, work and drive drunk after I got an automobile. Did I mention that I would have black outs? They were brutal! I remember being so high at a crack house one night that I just completely blacked out. When I finally regained consciousness, I looked around the room and saw a group a people *still* sitting around smoking crack. They made it seem okay, enabling me. So I got up in a dazed state of mind, I asked them to hand me the pipe, and I was back at it again. Are you getting a clear picture of the level of degradation associated with drug addiction and the depths of hell one descends to in this state of being?

Chapter 31- I Looked Up and Got Up

The fact of the matter is that no one will ever stop using drugs unless they want to do it themselves. No matter how much you want to prevent them from using by cutting off money, chasing after them, or blocking doors so that they cannot leave the house. Nothing will stop an addict from using until that addict wants something different; and that, in and of itself, may take many, many years. If you are a person of faith, the one thing you can and should always do is pray: keep them in your prayers.

One day I just got sick and tired of being sick and tired. I was tired of the traffic stops and citations with drug paraphernalia in my car. I was tired of living in utter darkness. I was tired of making drug runs and hoping to get back home without penalty. I was tired of the white demon's call and its aftermath. I was tired of the drunken stupors. I was tired of hurting those who loved me. I was just sick and tired of the whole seedy lifestyle.

That point started with a friend. I had a friend, and we used to smoke together, but we always said that we were going to quit. I knew that the only way that this individual would quit is if I would quit. She was my drug partner. We enabled each other to do *badly*. I was still drinking and having black outs during this time. But we encouraged each other to quit, and everything was going good until I relapsed. When I told her, and then saw her hit that pipe, the look of pain and disappointment on her face was unforgettable. I not only failed myself this time; I also failed her. This was *it* for me.

One day, I got on my knees and cried out to God to help me, because I really wanted to stop this addiction. I asked God to give me strength to get off of the drugs and alcohol. I haven't mentioned Him much, because although I knew He was always with me during my journey, *I obviously wasn't with Him*. There were no bells or whistles or thunder or lightning when I heard the voice of God in my spirit. It was just a knowing. I sensed in my spirit that God was guiding me to go to Alcoholics Anonymous (AA) meetings.

So I started attending AA meetings. But during the meetings, I would get convicted and feel uneasy, because they said that I had to leave the people, places and things that would hinder me from recovery. Like a shy kid in a new school, I felt anxious about such a sacrifice and vulnerability. They also said that I had to have a sponsor. I *tried* to follow things exactly the way they said it should be done. But to add to the discomfort, the meetings that I attended were composed of all white people, and I was the only black guy. The sponsor who they connected me with did not seem to want to be a part of my sobriety. He never called or followed up with me as a part of my AA sobriety plan. I felt out of place, but I knew this was God's instructions.

Later on, I felt convicted every time I went to the meetings, because I could not follow the AA program exactly as it was outlined. The reason I could not follow the plan the way it was outlined was because I could not quit my job at the nightclub as it was my whole livelihood. Furthermore, I could not bring myself to sacrifice all of the people, places and things that were required as a major part of the sobriety program in AA. However, the one thing that did work for me that I took away from AA was: "**No matter what, do not pick up** that first one."

I continued to follow that rule one day at a time. After my initial prayer, months went by before I realized that I was not having the same vicious cravings that plagued me for so long. Even more, that dark cloud that loomed over my head for so many years had suddenly dissipated.

It was a process. At first, days went by then months; before I knew it, I was sitting on years of freedom from the clutches of the white devil, the clutches of darkness. It was a miracle! This was God! His faithfulness proved true. After years of torment, God had delivered me from crack cocaine and alcohol all at once. Every craving and every desire was just gone; *done*. This miraculous testimony describes the smooth move of God, His power, His grace and His mercy to a lost soul like myself.

If I am able to tell anyone who has family members, friends, or anyone using drugs themselves one thing, it is that you cannot *just* pray it away. As I mentioned before, receiving prayers via having people stand in the gap for you goes a long way, but it is only just the cusp of what must transpire for one to vacate a drug habit completely. When it comes to quitting completely, the family member or friend cannot quit for the addict, and the addict cannot quit simply because it is the desire of the loved ones surrounding him or her. Addicts must have it in their hearts that they want to stop using drugs or drinking.

Today, I cannot even remember what it felt like to live a drug-infested lifestyle. All of the residue from that life is far gone. When God moved on my behalf, I did not have the earth-shattering experience as often depicted. Angels didn't sing from the heavens nor did I feel goosebumps all over my body, but the move of God came in a way that was appropriate for Tony. God did it in His own smooth way.

Thankfully, I am able to say that I have been drug and alcohol free for many years with no intention of looking or going back to the underworld. I am in the greatest shape of my life physically and mentally. I am expecting God to open doors for me to share my story on platforms around the world.

Chapter 32- How to Get Back Up When Life Knocks You Down

When Satan, in the form of crack cocaine, had control of my life, I was in a fight for my life. Life dealt me a number of knock-out blows. However, I thank God that I was fortunate enough to one day look up, take hold of His hand, and manage to get up on two feet. I had made the decision that being knocked, faced-down in the middle of the ring of life was not going to be my legacy.

There are things that may have occurred in your life that have dealt you a few knockout blows. Perhaps the opponents in your ring are not drugs or alcohol, but are still stiff opponents aimed to take you out and knock you down in life.

The most important lesson I learned in my fight with addiction was how to get back up when life knocks you down. The thing about landing on your back is, *"if you can look up, then you can get up"*, this is something Les Brown said for many years. However, you must **chose** to look up and get up. It's very easy, for us all, to lie there and wallow in the pits of despair, but the choice to change is a personal one.

Once back on your feet, the next step is to focus. You must look past your current position and on to your next move. You must think about the next swing you make. This requires a **focus** on your future. Begin to focus on where you want to go and who you want to be by beginning to redesign your life. Shake off what was, and embrace what is! Begin to enjoy the newness of life in a way that you never have before. I learned from boxing that focus is everything. You have to hone in on your opponent with eagle-eye precision because one mistake can prove to be fatal. Knockout blows are able to "stun," but God designed the brain with such elasticity, you are able to regain your focus, move on, and move up in life.

I can tell you from firsthand experience that you are obligated to persist! Quitting is not an option. **Persistence** is the key to victory. In the boxing ring one has to persist in order to emerge a winner. Sometimes it gets tough, you get tired, and want to give up, but you have to persist. You have to be relentless in the life arena in pursuing your goals, dreams and visions. Do not let anyone with a defeatist attitude stand in your way.

You must knock-out fear! **Fear** can never be a factor in your life. Fear immobilizes you so that you cannot move forward or backward. This nasty opponent, leaves you in a very uncomfortable neutral position and leaves you in a standstill position. You must take faith into the ring with you when you are facing fear. Faith annihilates fear. You must have faith in God and in your ability to do great things through Him.

When you have decided to get up from a nearly fatal knock-out blow, you get back up to do great things and live an extraordinary life. God has given you a second chance, and there is nothing to stop you now from achieving your heart's desires. In the boxing ring one cannot let their opponent perceive any hint of fear because in doing so, defeat is guaranteed. So in life, we must not let Satan sense any fear.

Every good boxer learns early in training how to follow-through on a good punch with a combination of solid blows. Now that you are back on your feet, you must set your combination of solid **follow-through** punches in the form of setting set goals and objectives for your life. Follow through with this technique until you have knocked out every one of the tasks that you set for yourself, and then start over again with new ones.

Great boxers know how to **look for openings** (opportunities) to deliver a good punch. In boxing, as well as in life, you have to look for openings. Look for opportunities that will work in your favor to accomplish and pursue the things that you desire in life. Look for those openings that will help you to move onward and upward. As much as it is perceived to be, opportunity is not standing at your door and knocking; rather, you have be prepared and aware to look for openings and go after them. Seize the moment to land that knock-out blow on an opportunity of a life-time.

Finally, the one thing that I failed to implement in my personal life was to ***roll with the punches***. I shared the story in this book about how my dad trained me to skillfully roll with the punches in the boxing ring and how those lessons served me well over the course of my boxing career. Unfortunately, it was clear that I did not apply that vital lesson to life.

In life, as with boxing, it is vitally important to learn the art of rolling with the punches. It is apparent that obstacles are sure to come your way, attempting to knock you off of your feet. At times, these punches aim to destroy you at your very core. They are meant to be fatal. Do not allow these punches to land! When swings come your way, and they will, learn how to ***roll with it and not give in to it***.

I am ***Tony "TNT" Tucker*** and I want you to know that you can get back up when life knocks you down. Not only can you get back up and stand strong, you can embark on a brand new journey. God has more in store for you than you can possibly imagine. Go after it and never look back! Do not even think about going back to any part of that life or anything or anyone associated with your past. It is a new day and brand new blessings are coming your way.

Contact Information

You have reached the end of this book. ***Thank you for reading***. If you have enjoyed what you read in this book, please tell a friend and send them to Tony's website for a link to purchase the book.

www.tonytnttucker.com

Gillespie Digital Media Group are masters of turning content into cash. We offer a suite of book writing, book publishing and book marketing services as well as webinar promotion and product creation. If you are ready to take the first step toward becoming a published author and reap the benefits of authorship and creating your own product, contact us today.

www.gillespiedigitalmediagroup.com
www.turncontentintocash.com

To book Mr. Tucker for celebrity appearances, speaking engagements, and/or product endorsements contact Gillespie Digital Media Group at 727-424-5934.

Made in the USA
Lexington, KY
12 January 2016